James E. Heg

Wisconsin County Asylums for the Chronic Insane

a paper read at the National Conference of Charities and Corrections

James E. Heg

Wisconsin County Asylums for the Chronic Insane
a paper read at the National Conference of Charities and Corrections

ISBN/EAN: 9783337837419

Printed in Europe, USA, Canada, Australia, Japan

Cover: Foto ©Suzi / pixelio.de

More available books at **www.hansebooks.com**

WISCONSIN

County Asylums

FOR THE

CHRONIC INSANE.

———

A paper read at the National Conference of Charities and Corrections by

JAMES E. HEG,

Member of Wisconsin State Board of Control.

MADISON, WISCONSIN:
DEMOCRAT PRINTING COMPANY, STATE PRINTER,
1896.

COUNTY CARE OF THE INSANE UNDER STATE SUPERVISION.

—

Certain facts have been established beyond a doubt in what is known as the " Wisconsin system," or county care of the insane under state supervision. They rest upon no hypothesis nor course of reasoning. They have gone into history and no attempt is made by any fair-minded or well informed man to contradict or question them even. It is upon these that we must rely, rather than suppositions, or theories, or wishes and the like. No clever hypotheses, no imposing array of venerable opinions, no plausibly constructed arguments, no abstruse scientific deductions may serve as a substitute for actual knowledge.

Disclaiming any professional knowledge in the care of the insane, and therefore unable to present plausible arguments or dogmatic theories on the subject, it will be all the more necessary for me to confine my statements entirely to facts that I know and about things I have seen. I shall speak only of the county care of the insane as understood in Wisconsin. Whether its success in Wisconsin is due to special laws or other causes not found elsewhere, I do not feel qualified to say, but its success has been demonstrated by fifteen years and the system is now a permanent institution of the state, which few would want to change.

The most humane and generous care of the insane, compatible with that economy rightly due to the tax payers, is the problem vexing the philanthropic mind nearly everywhere to-day and if the county care as exemplified in the

Wisconsin system is not a complete solution of the question, it comes nearer to it than any plan yet devised and proved.

This system rests upon two principles, Economy and Humanity, the true basic principles for the care of all our defective, delinquent and dependent classes. The present Wisconsin method of managing the insane was devised sixteen years ago by the State Board of Charities, now called Board of Control. In 1880, that board found in jails and poorhouses scattered throughout the state, 533 insane, crowded out of the hospitals, though the large northern hospital had been built only six years previously. The state hospitals were so overfilled that a new case could be received only by sending away an old one. Reports from many states show that the same condition of affairs exists to-day in nearly every state in the Union. Insanity increases much more rapidly than the ability of the people to pay for the erection of the expensive and pretentious palaces in which from 500 to 2,700 unfortunates can be herded and which cost from $1,000 to $2,500 per capita for the accommodations provided. Legislatures generally find so many needed avenues for the people's hard earned money that they cannot be blamed for not realizing as acutely as those who have immediate care of the insane, the great increase of people with minds diseased. In every state is heard the urgent cry for more hospital capacity, but alas, in how few of them is the cry heeded and relief given!

In the report of the Indiana conference of charities for 1895, the statement is made by Dr. S. E. Smith, in an argument for the state care of the insane, that there are about 700 insane in that state, "worthy of hospital care and treatment, yet denied this aid because the state has not made its accommodations keep pace with the needs." In a recent report of the Ohio board of charities the statement is made that in November, 1895, there were 1,422 insane in the county infirmaries or poor-houses of Ohio, the condition of whom was reported as truly pitiable. From a late report from New Jersey, made by the able secretary of the state board, Mrs. Williamson, we notice that 189 insane are kept in almshouses and a loud call for a reform in this line is made. The report of nearly every state we have been able to examine is of similar character or even worse, and this shows that state care of the insane does not mean the care of *all* the insane.

The condition of the 533 insane found in jails and poor-houses by the old State Board of Charities in 1880, was deplorable in the extreme. But the saddening record of humanity, neglect and brutality was in no wise different from that which could be told by any of you who are at all familiar with the care of the insane crowded out of the hospitals and asylums into jails and poor-houses. Raving maniacs were found in cells of jails where they had spent months, women were found literally in pens with no beds but loose straw, others were in cellars and basement cells, or chained to staples in the walls. The record is indeed sickening, but is it worse than can be seen even now in many states where state care of the insane is the policy?

The original intention of the Board of Charities was to provide for the 533 only, or rather to provide for the surplus insane who could not be cared for in the state hospitals. But the idea soon developed into the present system, which fifteen years has demonstrated to be eminently satisfactory. To-day Wisconsin has over 4,000 insane and not one of them is in a poor house or jail. And what is more, every insane person in the state is cared for. Can any other state say as much?

The law under which the Wisconsin county asylums for the chronic insane were organized was passed in 1881, and was entitled:

"An act to provide for the *humane* care of the chronic insane, not otherwise provided for."

It, in brief, provided that such counties as provide for their own chronic insane, *under such rules as the State Board of Charities should prescribe*, on the properly verified certificates of said board to the secretary of state, should receive the sum of $1.50 per week for each person so cared for.

The chronic insane only are provided for in these county asylums, while the hospitals are kept for the acute cases entirely. About 2,700 chronic insane are now being cared for in the 23 county asylums and fully as well cared for as in any state institution in the country. To have cared for these by the state would have required buildings that would have cost two million dollars. To have obtained that immense sum from the legislature would have been almost impossible and, if possible, would have entailed heavy burdens on the people.

For each person cared for in our state hospitals the county to which he belongs pays one dollar and fifty cents and his clothing bill to the state. For each inmate of a county asylum, the state pays the county $1 50. It will thus be seen that a county caring for its own insane really gets $3.25 a week in what it saves and what it receives. Three dollars and twenty-five cents a week is about as low as most state institutions in the country are able to care for their chronic insane. Very few, counting salaries, clothing, subsistence, fuel and repairs are as low even as this. The average weekly cost of keeping the insane in the county asylums, counting everything, is about $1.75, which makes an average gain of $1.50 per week for each inmate. Out of this gain, the counties that have had asylums ten or twelve years have paid for their entire permanent investment in land, buildings, improvements and repairs. In other words, the people have paid no more than they otherwise would have had to pay for the care of these insane in state institutions, yet have been able to save enough in twelve years to pay for their entire investment in handsome buildings, large farms, barns, and the like.

As a matter of economy could any better showing be made than this?

But some one says, "You must starve your insane to be able to make the weekly average as low as $1.75." By no means. I want to say right here that I have visited nearly all of these asylums at meal time, and I believe that the inmates are fully as well fed, if indeed not much better fed, as in any state asylum for chronics in the country. I have with me statements showing the dietary established in each county institution, which I shall be glad to have any one examine. I have verified the statements made in these papers and know that the facts are as represented.

Nearly all of the 23 asylums have a common dining room with seating capacity for all the inmates. With the kitchen adjoining, the food is served warm and in right condition. The tables of the dining room are covered with cloth and in season are graced with flowers. The walls have pictures and in general the room is the cheerful and pleasant apartment that it is in the ordinary home. Waiter girls, neatly attired, attend to the wants of the patients and see that every one has all he wants. Few homes have a more ample variety, more abundant supply and better cooked meals than one finds always in these county asylums.

Indeed, the inmates live fully as well as the average well-to-do American citizen, farmer or mechanic.

How is it that this can be done for $1.75 per week or less?

In the state hospitals, the cost per patient for wages and salaries is from $75 to $100 per year, while in the county asylums, with no expensive corps of officers, the average cost is about $26.50 per capita.

In the state hospitals, for subsistence the expense is about $65, while in the county asylums, the inmates being nearly all employed in some productive work, raising to a great extent the food consumed, the expense is but a trifle over $27 a year for each inmate.

In some of the county asylums the inmates make all of the clothing, shoes, etc., used and in all of them the women's clothing is made.

The county asylum farms contain from 80 to 500 acres of choice land. Such of the inmates as are able and willing to work — and a large percentage are both — help to raise the greater amount of the food consumed and this necessarily reduces the cost of the subsistence. And in these farms lies the secret of the beneficial results that are manifested from the county asylums. Occupation is found if possible for every inmate not entirely bed-ridden, with the result that the demented are roused from their stupor, the violent become calm and quiet, the filthy become cleanly and the physical condition of a large proportion is *decidedly* improved.

In nearly all of these asylums are hospital rooms for the sick, but there are so few at any one time that are ill that I have never yet seen any of these hospitals in use as such. A small bedroom off some ward is all that is necessary and is better when one is sick because more homelike and cheerful than the larger hospital apartment.

But it is not alone that the system is so economical that it is so well liked, but because it is the most humane plan yet devised and has accomplished results not dreamed of by the originators. In the first place, it permits the energies of the larger state hospitals to be devoted entirely to the cure of the curable, a consideration that must not be ignored. These hospitals are not weighed down with the care of a large number of unimprovable cases but are purely and wholly hospitals for the new cases of insanity in the fullest sense of the word.

Speaking of the condition in the Indiana state-care institutions Dr. Smith said in his paper before referred to, " The overcrowded wards prevent early and prompt admis- " sion of new cases. That delay in the treatment of the " acutely insane, under the most favorable surroundings,

'is harmful and diminishes the chances of safe recovery,
"will be denied by no one. Our first duty is to the cur-
'able insane and nothing should be omitted looking to a
restoration to health and useful citizenship."

On that principle we are working in Wisconsin. In the
work that is being done in its state hospitals, Wisconsin
takes great pride. We invite comparison with that wrought
in any other state for the scientific and progressive interest and investigation in the problems of practical psy-
chiatry and in the results upon the mind diseased.

The insane are committed first to the hospitals. So
long as there is any hope that hospital treatment can benefit either the mind or the body of the patient, he is kept
at the hospital, but when it is felt that there is no hope
for his recovery under existing conditions, the patient
is transferred to the county asylum nearest to his home
and relatives. The superintendent of the hospital and the
physician immediately in charge certify to the Board of
Control that the patient is eligible and suitable for transfer as being probably incurable. The Board of Control
then issues orders for his transfer. Notice of the transfer is sent by the superintendent of the hospital to the
relatives of the patient, who are free to visit him at the
asylum at nearly all times. One of the real benefits of the
system is that it educates the masses in the care of the
insane, in that it brings this unfortuante class closer to
the people. All of these asylums have large number of
visitors, some having as high as 100 a day, at times. All
of them have been obliged, in self defense, to forbid Sun-
day visits, but at other times there are few days that do
not bring some friends and relatives to the inmates. This
constant influx of visitors prevents the abuse or neglect
of inmates, even if there was a disposition to that effect.

We hear much from the state-care advocates about the
proverbial stinginess of the county boards in making ap-

propriations for these asylums. But as a matter of fact there has been no cause for complaint in Wisconsin.

The State Board of Control is the only medium through which a county can get any money from the state treasury, and, if this Board does its duty, there will be no trouble with the county authorities.

The State Board of Control is compelled by law to visit and inspect these asylums at least once every 90 days. Frequent visits are made without notice and at all times of the day. If the county authorities fail to properly care for the insane in any county asylum, the State Board can, and undoubtedly would, immediately transfer the insane in that asylum to some other institution, or it would withhold the payment of state money to the asylum until every·thing was arranged to the satisfaction of the Board. The superintendents of these asylums are very proud each of his own particular institution and all seem to be deeply in love with their work. They consult the State Board often and I have never found one who was not glad to receive official visits of inspection.

As a rule, the counties have been liberal with their ap·propriations for all purposes and have often given more money than is needed. The State Board and the local boards have worked in the greatest harmony and sugges·tions of the State Board are acted on with cheerfulness and alacrity. The local trustees are in nearly every instance the most prominent men in the county. They have the re·spect of their fellow-citizens to a marked degree and all of them take special interest in the work of these asylums. They know every inmate and the circumstances of each case. Their hearts are in the work and they give valu·able and splendid service to the cause of humanity.

There is considerable strife among the counties as to which shall build the next asylum needed and applications are before the Board at all times. The Board first grants permission to some county to build an asylum, limiting the capacity of the same, generally to 100 or 125. Then all plans for buildings are submitted to the Board for approval and changes are made in accordance with the suggestions of the Board. Some of the newer asylums are most beautiful structures, finished in hard woods, with an abundant supply of water, lighted by electricity and heated by steam. It has often been noticed, however, that the nearer to his normal condition the patient gets, the better is the result. The majority of the inmates come from very poor homes and to keep them in the palaces built for the insane in many of the states does not benefit the patients unaccustomed to such splendor and luxury.

The more homelike the buildings and rooms are, the less formality and restraint, the better the inmates get along, and the greater the chances appear for their recovery. Quite a number do recover. For the year ending March 1st of this year, there were 3⁵ recoveries, while fully 100 were absent on leave, visiting their old homes. More than 60 per cent. of the entire number of inmates were on parole and allowed to go about the farm without an attendant. Less than one per cent. were under restraint at any time. The doors are wide open all day and but few patients are kept on the wards.

Considerable stress is laid by the opponents of this system on the necessity of medical attendance. We go on the broad theory that there is nothing further that medical treatment can do for the diseased mind. All that can be done in the hospitals has been done. The physician is needed only for the ordinary and usual complaints of a similar number of normal people. A physician is appointed for each institution. He visits the same at regular and stated intervals, usually once or twice a week. In an emergency requiring the immediate services of a physician, he can be called by telephone in most asylums, and respond to a call in from fifteen minutes for the nearest to an hour for the farthest. Out of a total of about 2,800, there were 145 deaths for the year ending March 1st. Is the death rate at the state care institutions any less than this.

So far as I can learn, and so far as my observation goes, the amount of medical treatment which the chronic insane receive at the state-care asylums is limited to an autopsy and such treatment of physical infirmities as is always found in any large body of humanity, whether in or out of an asylum.

There can be, indeed, no question that with occupation for nearly every patient, with almost perfect liberty, open doors, no restraint of any sort, with general dining-room, home comforts of all kinds and personal individual attention absolutely essential to the insane, that there is a decided improvement in the mental as well as the physical condition of at least four-fifths of all those who are sent to these asylums. The secret lies in the plain fact that the insane are treated as human beings. The life of a patient in the county asylum is freer and less artificial than in the hospital. He is near to his people if they wish to see him. He has larger liberty and more labor. The simple life and healthful work of the farm induce vigor of muscle and tranquility of mind. The little remnant of intellect that each one has left is busied with the petty cares that each day brings. And thus in comparative serenity and peace, the flying years go by until one day the beautiful angel of death sets the clouded spirit free.

Allow me to add the testimony of one or two well posted gentlemen who have visited our county asylums and studied the system.

Hon. J. R. Elder, a member of the State Board of Charities of Indiana said in a paper to this Conference: "On "a visit to Wisconsin, I learned how they care for their "insane. That was a new development to me, to see one "hundred insane people in one building, men and women "taken from the poorhouses and state hospitals, in charge

"of one male and one female superintendent, doing all the
" work of the house and a large farm, with no doors locked,
" no resident physician, coming and going as they pleased,
' contented and as happy as they could be in their condition.
" Wisconsin has accomplished what other states must do.

More than half of the present inmates in our state hos-
" pitals could be cared for in this way-better for the harm-
" less insane, much better and cheaper for the state."

So great an authority as Hon. F. B. Sanborn of Massa-
chusetts, who has made a full and thorough study of this
question, said to this conference in 1892:

" I make the assertion and I challenge any one to prove
" the contrary that the state of Wisconsin comes at this
" moment nearer to the ideal standard of providing for
" every person the treatment best adapted to his needs
" than any state in the Union. I have studied this matter
" for years, have watched and examined the Wisconsin sys-
" tem, and have repeatedly stated (and it has never been
" disproved) that the insane of Wisconsin are better provided for in all the essentials of treatment than the in-
" sane of any other state."

In order to settle this question, however, I would here-
with urge this Conference to appoint a committee to visit
as many of our 23 county asylums as may be possible, talk
with the inmates, examine into the dietary, the work and
daily life of these institutions, and make a report of their
investigations to the next Conference.

The State Board of Control of Wisconsin will do all in
its power to make such investigation complete and thorough and will aid this committee in every possible way.

14

Statement showing total cost, acres in farms, and cost of same, number of inmates and where from, and average cost per capita in county asylums of Wisconsin for year ending Sept. 30, 1895.

County Asylum.	Total cost, exclusive of farm.	Acres in farm.	Cost of farm.	Number of inmates from own county.	Number of inmates from other counties.	Total number of inmates.	Average cost per capita per week.
Brown...........	$10,073 08	113	$5,000 00	86	23	109	$1 80
Chippewa (not opened until 1896)	54,785 15	210	7,000 00				
Columbia......	28,489 43	200	5,200 00	49	52	101	1 32
Dane..........	52,542 90	485	24,250 00	130	17	147	1 18
Dodge.........	43,909 64	220	17,000 00	74	41	115	1 85
Dunn..........	80,831 58	420	10,500 00	46	92	138	1 53
Fond du Lac...	59,855 96	55	5,800 00	97	32	129	1 96
Grant	41,635 49	423	21,150 00	71	39	110	1 72
Green	42,294 50	320	12,000 00	65	48	113	1 73
Iowa	49,120 61	420	18,600 00	52	61	113	1 65
Jefferson......	71,500 28	182	12,000 00	72	43	115	1 79
La Crosse.....	84,788 13	320	8,225 00	69	49	118	1 39
Marathon.....	89,754 38	235	5,000 00	31	112	143	1 67
Manitowoc ...	49,948 37	173	15,900 00	61	60	121	1 77
Milwaukee.....	85,807 11	40	20,000 00	126		126	2 48
Outagamie ...	76,901 08	335	18,023 90	62	54	116	1 47
Racine........	62,905 82	144	10,343 75	76	46	122	1 95
Rock..........	143,559 32	380	38,000 00	108	28	136	1 58
Sauk..........	26,994 88	165	7,000 00	45	43	88	1 35
Sheboygan.....	54,882 05	40	6,000 00	85	24	109	1 90
Vernon........	60,051 70	230	8,200 00	47	73	120	1 63
Walworth......	29,516 15	240	9,600 00	64	31	95	1 12
Winnebago.....	99,964 49	291	14,259 00	102	56	158	1 93
Totals....	$1,420,172 10	5,674	$299,051 65	1,618	1,024	2,642